I0753080

N is for Noah's Ark

Dr. C's LEARN the BIBLE SERIES

Dr. C. White-Elliott

www.clfpublishing.org
909.315.3161

Cover design by Senir Design. Contact info: info@senirdesign.com

ISBN # 978-1-945102-66-0

Printed in the United States of America.

Dedicated to

Ny’lex Garyelle Jones

There was once a man named Noah. In God's eyes, Noah was a good man. When God decided it was time for the first rain, He told Noah to build an ark from cypress wood. God told Noah how long and how wide the ark should be. And, Noah followed God's instructions.

It had never rained before, so Noah and his family did not know what to expect. All they knew was when the rain came, the earth would be flooded with water. The earth and all the people would be destroyed. But, the ark would keep Noah and his family safe.

Noah and his family were the only people who would go inside the ark. Everyone else would be left to deal with the rain and the destruction that would follow. They didn't believe Noah when he told them about the rain. They laughed at him.

Although many people made fun of him, Noah and his family worked very hard. They believed God and His warning, and they were obedient to His instructions about building the ark.

It took Noah many, many years to build the ark. When he was finished, it was a beautiful sight to see. It was huge, and there were many levels inside that would be used for different supplies and the animals it would soon carry.

Not long after, it was time to gather the animals and take them inside for shelter. Noah took at least one male and one female of each type of animal and of each type of bird.

Not long after every member of Noah's family was aboard the ark with all the animals, the rain came. It rained for 40 days. Soon, the land was covered in water, and the ark began to float.

The water stayed on the earth for 150 days. Then, Noah sent a dove out, and the dove returned to him with an olive branch. That was a sign that there was new growth and that the water had begun to go down.

After the dove returned, Noah and his family knew it was safe to exit the ark. They let all the animals out, so they would be free to roam the land as they had done before.

When everyone had come out from the ark, they saw that there were no other people. They had all died in the flood. And, God's heart was heavy. So, He sent a sign: a beautiful rainbow, to show He would never destroy the earth again with water. Always remember, when you see a beautiful rainbow, it is a message from God, showing us how much He loves us and to remind us of His promise.

www.ingramcontent.com/pod-product-compliance
Lightning Source LLC
LaVergne TN
LVHW071630100826
845154LV00007BA/119

9781945102660